Reading STREET
Grade K

Scott Foresman

Practice Book 3
Teacher's Manual
Unit 3

PEARSON
Scott Foresman

Editorial Offices: Glenview, Illinois • Parsippany, New Jersey • New York, New York
Sales Offices: Needham, Massachusetts • Duluth, Georgia • Glenview, Illinois
Coppell, Texas • Sacramento, California • Mesa, Arizona

ISBN: 0-328-14526-2

Contents

Unit 3
Watch Me Change

Color the /n/ pictures red and /b/ pictures blue.

You are your child's first teacher!

This week we're ...

Reading *Little Panda*

Talking About Animals Grow and Change

Learning About Connect /n/ to *Nn* and /b/ to *Bb*
Compare and Contrast

Here are ways to help your child practice
skills while having fun!

Day 1 | **Read Together**
Write n on one card and b on another card. Have
your child show the correct card when you say the
following words: *nap, bat, bib, nine, Bob,* and *Nan.*

Day 2 | **Read Together**
Have your child read the Phonics Story *Nan and
Nick.* Find words with /n/ and /b/. Have your child
name the /n/ and /b/ words on page 4.

Day 3 | **Connect /n/ to *Nn* and /b/ to *Bb***
Have your child add the letter *n* or *b* to make
words.

_ap   _in   _at   _an

Day 4 | **Verbs**
Act out the following words with your child: *jump,
skip, sit, eat,* and *drink.* After each action, ask your
child what you did. Tell your child that these words
are verbs.

Day 5 | **Practice Handwriting**
Have your child practice writing *n* and *b* words.

bed   Ned   bat   Bob

2

Words to talk about

weigh	measure	healthy
bamboo	curious	explore

Words to read

me	with	she
pan	bit	pin
bin	nap	bib

3

Name _____

 Write  Color

 n    n

 n    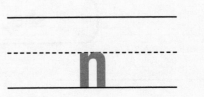 Nn

n

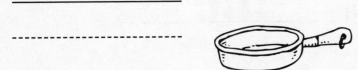   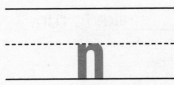 n 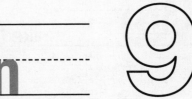 9

 Directions: Name each picture. Write *n* on the line if the word begins with /n/. Color the /n/ pictures.

 Home Activity: Have your child name other words that begin with /n/.

© Pearson Education K

Name _____

 **Write**  **Color**

| she | with | me | we |

_____

Pam ran  me.

_____

 ran to the mat.

_____

We like to run.

_____

Run with me.

 Directions: Write the missing word to finish each sentence. Color the pictures.

 Home Activity: Have your child use *me, with,* and *she* in other sentences.

4 **High-Frequency Words**

Practice Book Unit 3

Nat sat.

Nan sat with Nat.

Phonics Story *Nan and Nat*
Target Skill Consonant *Nn/n/*

Nan and Nat

Nan ran with a net.

She ran to Nat.

Nan is with Nat.

Nat ran with a net.

2

Nat ran with the net.

Nan ran with the net.

3

Name _____

 # Color

 Directions: Color each matching pair a different color.

 School + Home **Home Activity:** Have your child compare and contrast two family members.

Name _____

 Write  Color

n green	**b** blue	**n** green
b blue	**n** green	**b** blue

 Directions: Name each picture. Write the letter for the final sound in the box. Color final /n/ words green and final /b/ words blue.

School + Home **Home Activity:** Have your child trace *n* and *b* and name the pictures.

8 **Phonics** Consonants *Nn*/n/ and *Bb*/b/

© Pearson Education K

Name _____

 Color

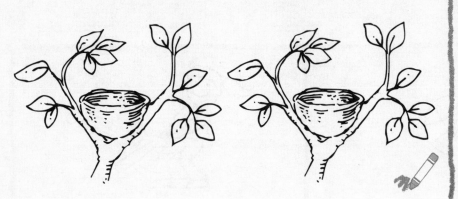

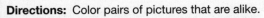 **Directions:** Color pairs of pictures that are alike.

School + Home **Home Activity:** Have your child tell how the pairs of pictures are alike or different.

Practice Book Unit 3

Comprehension Compare and Contrast **9**

Circle  **Color**

run

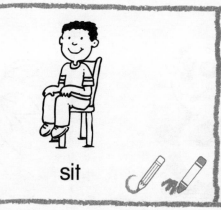

sit

net

dig

ball

hit

 Directions: Name the pictures. Circle and color each verb.

 Home Activity: Have your child name other action words.

Help Ron find his way home by following the path with /r/ animals.

4

Family Times

You are your child's first teacher!

This week we're ...

Reading *Little Quack*

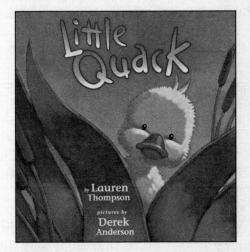

Talking About Learning to Do New Things

Learning About Connect /r/ to *Rr*
Plot

1

Here are ways to help your child practice skills while having fun!

Day 1

Read Together

Read the following sentence to your child: *I like to run and read.* Ask your child to name the /r/ words in the sentence. Continue with this sentence: *I like to ride and rake.*

Day 2

Read Together

Have your child read the Phonics Story *Rob the Rat.* Find /r/ words.

Day 3

Connect /r/ to *Rr*

Have your child name the /r/ words on page 4. Then have him or her replace the first letter of each word with the letter *r* to make a new word.

bug   man   sip

Day 4

Verbs

Have your child tell you what he or she did at school today. Tell your child that the words used to say what he or she did are called verbs. Have your child use verbs to tell things to do after school.

Day 5

Practice Handwriting

Have your child copy the sentence. Tell your child that *ran* and *race* are /r/ words. Also, remind your child that *ran* is a verb.

I ran the race.

2

Words to talk about

| duckling | pond | paddle |
| plunged | proud | brave |

Words to read

me	with	she
ran	rib	rip
bit	bat	bin

3

Name _____

 Write  **Color**

_____

_____
r

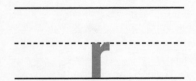

_____

_____
r

Rr

_____

_____

_____

_____
r

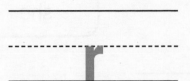 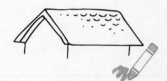

_____

_____

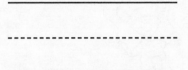 

_____

_____
r

 Directions: Name each picture. Write *r* on the line if the word begins with /r/. Color the /r/ picture.

 Home Activity: Find pictures that begin with /r/. Paste the pictures on paper to make an /r/ book.

Name _____

 Write  Color

| she with me little |

_____

She can jump rope.

_____

She can run **with** me.

_____

She can hop with **me** .

_____

This is a **little** duck.

 Directions: Write the missing word to finish each sentence. Color the pictures.

 Home Activity: Have your child use the *she, with,* and *me* in other sentences.

© Pearson Education K

Rin the Rat

Rin is a rat.

She is a little rat.

Rin ran to Rip.

Rip ran.

Phonics Story *Rin the Rat*
Target Skill Consonant *Rr*/r/

Rin likes to tap.

She can tap.

Rip can see Rin.

He looks at Rin.

Name _____

Directions: Color the picture that shows what would happen next in each story.

School + Home **Home Activity:** Have your child count the ducklings in each picture.

Name _____

 Color 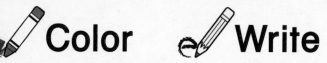 Write

 Directions: Color the pictures that begin with /r/. Write *r* in the box.

School + Home **Home Activity:** Have your child name the pictures that begin with /r/.

Name _____

Draw

Directions: Draw a picture to show what would happen next in each story.

Home Activity: Ask your child to recall what happened at school today, telling the events in order.

Name _____

Draw

run

swim

eat

fly

Directions: Read each verb. Draw a picture to show the action.

Home Activity: Have your child tell about their action word pictures.

20 **Grammar** Verbs

Practice Book Unit 3

Circle the /k/ pictures. Color the /d/ pictures.

Family Times

You are your child's first teacher!

This week we're ...

Reading   *See How We Grow*

Talking About   Children Change as They Grow

Learning About   Connect /d/ to *Dd* and /k/ to *Kk*
Cause and Effect

Here are ways to help your child practice skills while having fun!

Day 1 | **Listen for /d/ and /k/**

Read the following words to your child. Tell your child to dance if /d/ is heard and kick if /k/ is heard: *dog, deer, key, kite, dime,* and *king.*

Day 2 | **Read Together**

Have your child read the Phonics Story *Pit Did!* Find /d/ and /k/ words. Ask your child to name the /d/ and /k/ words on page 4.

Day 3 | **Connect /d/ to *Dd* and /k/ to *Kk***

Have your child look for objects that begin with /d/ or /k/. Have your child point to the items and say the names.

Day 4 | **Verbs that add -s**

Say the word *walk.* Tell your child that sometimes the letter *s* is added to the verb to fit in a sentence. When *s* is added, the word *walk* becomes *walks.* Have your child add *s* to each of these words: *run, ride, jump, skip.*

Day 5 | **Practice Handwriting**

Have your child copy the words *dance, kick,* and *dash.* Tell your child that these are verbs.

Words to talk about

twins	newborn	crawl
walk	children	babies

Words to read

see	look	me
dad	kid	Kim
kit	dab	Dan

2

3

Name _____

 Write   Color

_____
d   
_____

_____
d   
_____

_____

_____

Dd

_____

_____

_____
d   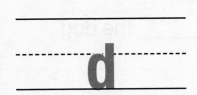
_____

_____
d   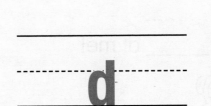
_____

Directions: Name each picture. Write *d* on the line if the word begins with /d/. Color the /d/ pictures.

© Pearson Education K

 School + Home   **Home Activity:** Find pictures that begin with /d/. Paste the pictures on paper to make an /d/ book.

Name _____

 Write  Color

see   look

_____
I can ___ **see** ___ the cat.

_____
I ___ **look** ___ for my cat.

_____
___ **Look** ___ at me!

_____
Pat can ___ **see** ___ the dog.

 Directions: Write the missing word to finish each sentence. Color the pictures.

 Home Activity: Have your child use the high-frequency words in other sentences.

© Pearson Education K

Pit ran to the dish.

Pit did.

Phonics Story *Pit Did!*
Target Skill Consonant *Dd*/d/

Name _____

Pit Did!

Pit can see duck.

Pit ran with the duck.

Pit did.

Pit can see the doll.

Pit ran to the doll.

2

Pit can look at the door.

Pit ran to the door.

Pit did.

3

Name _____

 Draw  Color

 Directions: Draw a line from what happened to why it happened. Color each picture.

 Home Activity: Have your child tell why each event happened.

Comprehension Cause and Effect **27**

© Pearson Education K

Name _____

 **Write**   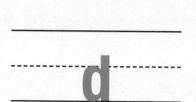 **Color**

_____
- - - - - - - - - - - - - - - -
k
_____

_____
- - - - - - - - - - - - - - - -
d
_____

_____
- - - - - - - - - - - - - - - -
d
_____
 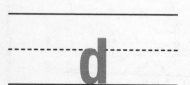

Kk
Dd

_____
- - - - - - - - - - - - - - - -
d
_____

_____
- - - - - - - - - - - - - - - -
k
_____
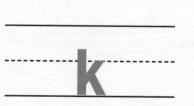 

_____
- - - - - - - - - - - - - - - -
k
_____
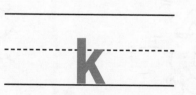 

 Directions: Name each picture. Write *k* or *d* on the line if the word begins wih /k/ or /d/. Color the pictures.

 Home Activity: Have your child find other words that begin with /k/ or /d/.

Name _____

 Draw  Color

 Directions: Draw a line from what happened to why it happened. Color each picture.

 Home Activity: Have your child tell you what happened in each picture and why it happened.

Practice Book Unit 3

Comprehension Cause and Effect **29**

Name _____

 Write   Color

jump   **jumps**

run   **runs**

walk   **walks**

 Directions: Add -s to each verb. Write the word. Then draw a line to the action picture. Color each picture.

School + Home

Home Activity: Have your child read each sentence.

30   **Grammar** Verbs That Add -s

Practice Book Unit 3

Color the pictures that begin with /f/.

Family Times

You are your child's first teacher!

This week we're ...

Reading *Farfallina & Marcel*

Talking About   Friendships Change

Learning About   Connect /f/ to *Ff*
Plot

Here are ways to help your child practice skills while having fun!

Day 1 **Read Together**

Play the "I see something..." game with your child. For example, say, "I see something that swims in the water. Guess something that starts with /f/." Continue with other /f/ items, such as *fork, fan,* and *fox.*

Day 2 **Read Together**

Have your child read the Phonics Story *For Me!* Find words that have /f/.

Day 3 **Connect /f/ to Ff**

Ask your child to name the /f/ words on page 4. Then have your child choose another book. Look for /f/ words in the story. Work together to name other words that begin with /f/.

Day 4 **Verbs**

Ask your child to name verbs for things to do on the weekends. Tell your child that verbs have different endings if the action has already happened. Give some examples, such as *talk* and *talked, race* and *raced.*

Day 5 **Practice Handwriting**

Have your child write the letter *f* in the blanks to form new words.

_it   _an   _in

Words to talk about

| goose | gosling | caterpillar |
| butterfly | reflection | cocoon |

Words to read

see	look	fin
did	fan	fit
rip	rat	kit

Name _____

 Write    **Color**

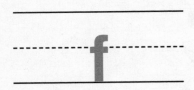 f

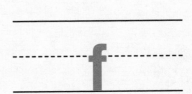

 f

 Ff

 f

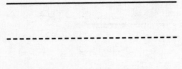

 f

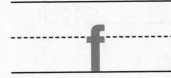

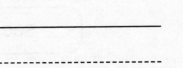

 Directions: Name each picture. Write *f* on the line if the word begins with /f/. Color the pictures.

 Home Activity: Find pictures that begin with /f/. Paste the pictures on paper to make an /f/ book.

© Pearson Education K

Name _____

 Write  Color

| see | look | with | for |

_____

I can ___**see**___ the bird.

_____

It is ___**for**___ the cat.

_____

I can ___**look**___ for it.

_____

Mom can run ___**with**___ me.

 Directions: Write the missing word to finish each sentence. Color the pictures.

 Home Activity: Have your child use the high-frequency words in other sentences.

34 **High-Frequency Words**

Practice Book Unit 3

I see a fin for me.

Look at the fin.

For Me!

I see a fan for me.

Look at the little fan.

I see a fox for me.

Look at the little fox.

2

I see a fish for me.

Look at the fish.

3

Name _____

Number

3

1

2

 Directions: Have children number the pictures to tell the beginning, middle, and end of the story.

 Home Activity: Have your child summarize the plot of the story.

© Pearson Education K

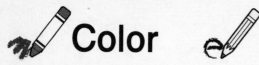 Color  Write

 Directions: Name each picure. Color the pictures that begin with /f/. Write f in the box.

 Home Activity: Have your child name the pictures that begin with /f/.

38 **Phonics** Consonant *Ff/f/*

Practice Book Unit 3

© Pearson Education K

Name _____

Number Color

2

1

3

2

3

1

 Directions: Number the pictures in each row to show the beginning, middle, and end of the story. Color the picture that shows the end of the story.

 Home Activity: Have your child summarize the plot.

Practice Book Unit 3

Comprehension Plot **39**

Name _____

Read  Color

sat

walks

jumps

looks

ran

sees

 Directions: Read the word. Color the pictures that show something is happening now.

 Home Activity: Have your child tell about the pictures and identify what is happening now and what has happened.

40 **Grammar** Verbs for Now and the Past

© Pearson Education K

Practice Book Unit 3

Color pictures with /o/.

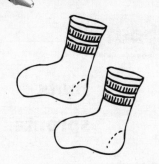

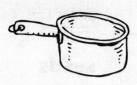

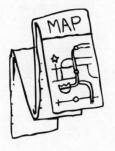

Family Times

You are your child's first teacher!

This week we're ...

Reading *Seeds*

Talking About Plants Grow and Change

Learning About Connect /o/ to *Oo*
Draw Conclusions

4

1

Here are ways to help your child practice skills while having fun!

Day 1 **Read Together**

Read the following sentence to your child. Have your child hop every time an /o/ is heard. Use the picture names on page 4 to continue the activity.

Tom dropped the hot pot.

Day 2 **Read Together**

Have your child read the Phonics Story *Little Fox*. Find words that have /o/.

Day 3 **Connect /o/ to Oo**

Have your child fill in the blanks with the letter *o*. Then have your child find the three rhyming words.

d_t   m_p   h_t   R_n   p_t

Day 4 **Meaningful Word Groups**

Ask your child the following question: *"Did you go to school today?"* Ask him or her to respond with a sentence such as, *"Yes, I went to school today."* Have your child create answers to other questions you ask.

Day 5 **Practice Handwriting**

Have your child complete the sentence. Then have him or her copy the sentence.

My name is _____.

Words to talk about

seeds	pod	roots
stem	pit	sprouts

Words to read

they	you	of
mop	top	Ron
dot	not	fin

Name _____

 Color 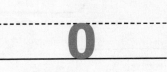 Write

_____

octopus

_____

O

_____

igloo

Oo

_____

ox

O

_____

otter

O

_____

olives

O

_____

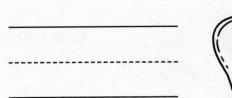

apple

 Directions: Name each picture. Write *o* on the line if the word begins with /o/. Color the /o/ pictures.

 Home Activity: Look through a newspaper or book with your child and point out words that begin with *Oo*.

Practice Book Unit 3

Phonics Short *Oo*/o/ **43**

© Pearson Education K

Name _____

 Write  Color

| they | of | you | she |

_____

Can _____**she**_____ see you?

It is a lot _____**of**_____ fun.

_____

Can _____**you**_____ see the top?

_____**They**_____ can see the fox.

 Directions: Write the missing word to finish each sentence. Color the pictures.

 Home Activity: Have your child use the high-frequency words in other sentences.

Little Rob is not sad.

Little Rob can have the top.

4

Phonics Story *Little Rob*
Target Skill Short *Oo*/o/

Name _____

Little Rob

Little Rob is sad.

He is little.

1

Little Rob is on a mat.

He is sad.

Little Rob can see a top.

Can he have the top?

Name _____

 Circle  Color

 Directions: Circle the picture that shows what you think the child would do next. Color the picture.

 Home Activity: Have your child explain how they arrived at their conclusion.

Practice Book Unit 3

Name _____

 Write  Color

_____

o

_____

o

_____

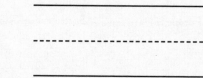 Oo

_____

o

 Directions: Name each picture. Write *o* on the line if the word has middle /o/. Color the /o/ pictures.

 School + Home **Home Activity:** Make a list of words with /o/.

Name _____

 Circle  **Color**

She is _____.

 mad

sad

glad

She is _____.

mad

 sad

glad

 Directions: Circle the word to finish the sentence.
Color the pictures.

Home Activity: Have your child tell why he or she
drew the conclusion he or she did.

Practice Book Unit 3

Comprehension Draw Conclusions **49**

Read Draw

We have a bat.

Rob can mop.

It is a fan.

Directions: Read each sentence. Draw a picture that shows the meaning of each sentence.

 Home Activity: Have your child read each sentence and tell about their pictures.

Circle the pictures with /o/.

Family Times

You are your child's first teacher!

This week we're ...

    Reading *Hide Clyde!*

Talking About Changing for Protection

Learning About Connect /o/ to *Oo*
                       Main Idea

Here are ways to help your child practice skills while having fun!

Day 1 **Read Together**

Have your child name the items on page 4 that have /o/. Then have your child talk about the items in a sentence, such as, *"This is a sock."*

Day 2 **Read Together**

Have your child read the Phonics Story *A Hat for Tom.* Find words that have /o/.

Day 3 **Connect /o/ to Oo**

Put a *dot* on a card. Have your child show the *dot* each time you say a word with /o/. Say these words *hot, stop, sled, pot, top, cap, mop, lock.*

Day 4 **Sentences**

Tell your child that a sentence has *a naming part* and *an action part*. Say the sentence, *The bunny hopped.* Ask your child to tell the naming part and the action part. Continue with other sentences.

Day 5 **Practice Handwriting**

Have your child fill in the blanks with the letter *o*. Then have your child repeat the sentence after you.

The f_x was h_t.

2

Words to talk about

chameleon	jungle	pattern
skin	hide	scampered

Words to read

they	you	of
rod	Tom	pot
cot	dot	fan

3

Name _____

 Write    Color

f o x

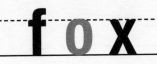

t o p

c a p

m o p

 **Oo**

b i b

b o x

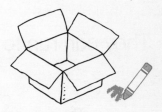

 Directions: Write o, a, or i to finish each word. Color the /o/ pictures.

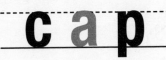 **Home Activity:** Have your child write *mop* and *map* and draw a picture for each word.

© Pearson Education K

Name _____

 Write  Color

| they | of | you | we |

_____

We can see the dog.

_____

I see a lot **of** dogs.

_____

They can run to **you** .

_____

They ran to me.

 Directions: Write the missing word to finish each sentence. Color the pictures.

 Home Activity: Have your child use the high-frequency words in other sentences.

It is not on the rat.

It is in the pot.

Phonics Story *A Cap for Tom*
Target Skill Short Oo/o/

A Cap for Tom

Tom can have a cap.

Is the cap on Tom?

The cap is not on Tom.
See the cap.

The cap is not on Tom.
It is on the rat.

Name _____

 Color

Directions: Color the picture that illustrates the main idea of the story *Hide Clyde!*

School + Home **Home Activity:** Have your child tell how chameleons hide to protect themselves.

Name _____

 Circle  Color

fix fox		map mop	
cab cob		tap top	

 Directions: Circle the word that names the picture.
Color the /o/ pictures.

 Home Activity: Have your child draw a picture of an /o/ word.

Name _____

 Color

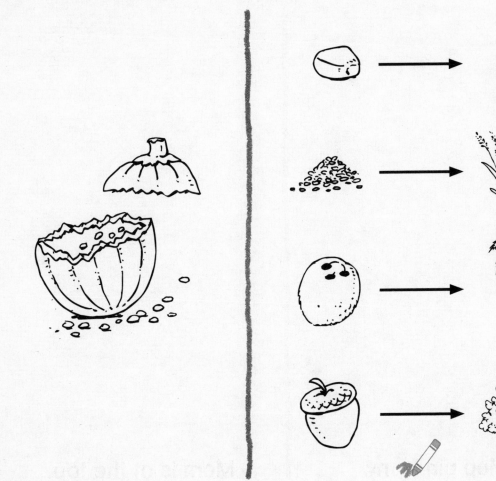

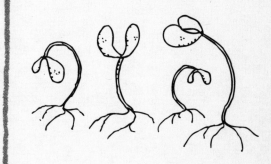

🍎 **Directions:** Color the picture that illustrates the main idea.

 School + Home **Home Activity:** Have your child tell about each picture.

Comprehension Main Idea **59**

Name _____

Read  Draw

Ron can see the rod.

Mop pin is my.

Mom is at the top.

 Directions: Read the words. If the words make a sentence, draw a picture that shows the meaning of the sentence.

 Home Activity: Have your child read each sentence and tell which words do not make a sentence.

60 **Grammar** Sentences